INVADING YOUR PRIVACY
What You Don't Know &
What You Should Know

I0436387

CreateSpace edition
2nd edition

Table Of Contents

Introduction

Many Americans take for granted that we have a legal protection of our personal privacy. They might be surprised to learn that the US Constitution offers no such specific assurances. Yes, the framers did include a Bill of Rights with its related provisions in this area. Among them are...
...privacy of beliefs (*1st Amendment*)
...privacy of a home against demands that it be used to house soldiers (*3rd Amendment*)
...privacy of a person and possessions against unreasonable searches (*4th Amendment*)
...privacy of personally held information... aka the privilege against self-incrimination (*5th Amendment*)

With this in mind we may mistakenly construe that our personal information is being well protected by the force of law. However, nothing could be further from the truth. While no one can compel us to reveal our secrets (*except by granting immunity or by the threat of contempt of court*), this is exactly what we do "voluntarily" on a routine basis. You might be amazed to see how pervasive this dissemination of personal information really is.

Business Intrusion

What we may think of as our private information can come to light as not being private when our personal transactions take place in the public domain, such as through...
...banking
...borrowing
...purchasing
...using the courts
...the Internet

And nearly all of this personal information is being recorded by a vast number of companies who make this data 'their own business' in order to sell it to a wide range of interested parties, including to the federal and state governments. These companies who do the data capturing and aggregating maintain immense quantities records on virtually all of us. Their databases include the billions of public transaction that take place on a regular basis. It is collected, collated, and served up to the myriad of buyers who may glean, among other things, what are our…

…birth records
…home address and phone numbers
…family structure
…religious preferences
…individual and family income
…buying habits (*especially*)
…real estate records
…mortgage debt
…political affiliation
…voting records
…offenses that may have been committed
…court involvement history

If you are willing to cough up their fees, the amount of data that one can find on virtually anyone is staggering.

Ever since George Orwell's classic book dealing with the perils of big brother government, there have been the occasional, dire warnings from a handful of citizens regarding the adverse consequences of having such power concentrated in the databanks of those who would make use of it.

For years we have been warned of this increasing encroachment into our private lives, and the warnings have gone mostly unheeded by the general public. Sure there are a number of fringe groups that attempt to expose the evils of the state and business, but they too are largely ignored. That is unless they address their grievances with violent or illegal action. Along with their paranoia comes their imagined repression by government, which further serves to fuel their extremist beliefs. Need I mention the White Supremacist or the NRA as groups that seriously or loosely falling into this mindset?

Who would have thought that it would be our businesses and our criminal elements, rather than just our government, who are leading the assault on our being left to live in peace and quiet? Forget for the moment the malicious computer hackers that try to inflict harm for their monetary advantage. Targeted business ads and click-tracking on the Internet are pervasive, and this encroachment is trending ever more in that direction. When you browse anywhere on the net there is invariably software which wants to know what you are buying and what your surfing habits are in order to target you for their sales ad invasions of your computer screen.

A recent "big-brother" exposé revealed that Google has kept a record of every inquiry that has ever made by every person who used their search engine. While they claim that they have no nefarious motive for this failure to delete, they are not spending millions or billions of dollars on data storage for nothing. It is only a matter of time before they decide to sell this data to those companies who will use it to pigeonhole our activities for whatever motives they might have. And the folks at Google had the brass to lobby (*successfully*) to have their company excluded from a recent privacy protection law. And how did this happen? Follow the lobbyist money.

In 2011 MasterCard and Visa announced their intentions to tie their vast databases of credit card purchases to each cardholder's online experiences for the purpose of targeted advertising. These product connections would then be sold to other companies so that they could then provide ads that reflect people's implied interests. For example, if you subscribed to an automobile magazine, you might be subjected to receiving car ads on your browser. While the technical details of this new form of database mining had not been worked out as of this writing, the handwriting is on the wall.

In 2011 Fair Isaac (*the folks who brought us the FICO credit scoring*) announced that they are branching out into the new area (*for them*) of understanding human behaviors. This is not an intellectual quest, but rather it involves being able to determine sophisticated ways that can predict our actions in order to sell that information to those companies which will use it to their advantage for advertising purposes.

I suppose there are some who will not consider these probes into our lives to be much of an invasion of privacy. Perhaps they can even be viewed as being an improvement on the annoying, pointless ads we are now inundated with.

For those of you who cherish your smartphones, there is a growing risk of being tracked when you visit the mall. These phones have a hardware-imbedded MAC (media access control) address in them that is accessible when the phone is turned on. This would permit stores with the right electronics to trace some people's movements throughout a shopping center.

While the industry claims that they can not connect an individual person to a phone, how difficult do you think it would it be to uncover and add your MAC to their store accounts whenever you make a purchase. Not difficult at all, I suspect. Then they would have the usable connection between a phone and a person.

Government Intrusion

When I joined the Air Force many years ago I was surprised to learn that they were aware of a traffic ticket that I had received. Now if this personal information could be so easily obtained by a government entity before computerization took hold, what do you think today's snooping capabilities are?

In 2012 the feds announced their future plans to have "black boxes" installed in all cars and light trucks. Ostensibly this tracking of various driving parameters, such as speed and steering position, etcetera, would be used to make driving safer or to allow the police to assign blame in the case of an accident. But this potentially useful information may not prevent insurance companies from accessing the data after an accident. It could then be used to modify or cancel your policy with them. Stay tuned on this one.

In 2012 the Wall Street Journal reported that the latest "crime fighting technique" that is increasingly being used by law enforcement is the license plate scanning of immense numbers of cars that take to our roads and highways. Even while an officer is parked in his police vehicle doing paperwork or writing a ticket, his computerized equipment can be automatically scanning every parked car plate in the vicinity, as well as those that drive by.

While the courts have not ruled against the use of this surveillance procedure to date, it is clearly an invasion of privacy since these devices could be used to track an innocent driver's...
...parked locations
...their coming and goings
...the time of day that is attached to each record

It may not have occurred yet, but these records can then be "mined" to reveal a person's habits without the consent of a judge. I personally think this falls into the unreasonable search category.

We have been warned time and again about the potential and the reality of unwarranted government intrusions into our lives. With each erosion of our privacy there have been those who seek to justify it. Mostly this small but powerful crowd of infringement supporters is made up of those who have or would benefit from these incursions. Sometimes it may simply be well meaning, sometimes not.

One of the potentially scarier innovations of the digital age is the computerized technique of facial recognition. This could become an issue when you post pictures of yourself on the Internet. They can be digitized, stored, and later used with other captured images of you going about your business or shopping. Correlations can then be made that reveal your habits. Eventually what you do, where you go, and maybe even what you think will be in a database here, there, and who knows where.

Big brother is just getting into high gear thanks to the data appetite of big business in conjunction with their efforts to pigeonhole your likes and dislikes. Unfortunately they do not take our aversion to invasion of privacy as an important disturbance. Today this is done to sell you more products. Tomorrow, who knows what evil lurks in the hearts of men. It would be naïve to think that this future is not more serious than howling at the wind.

Press Intrusion

Not many of us will suffer from the presses' insatiable thirst for salacious news, that is 'unless we are a celebrity of some sort. But common folks can also be subjected to their *news at any price'* mentality. Anyone who makes a headline, whether large or small, can become the interest of the press for their own purposes.

In late 2013 a Phoenix AZ newspaper and a television station joined forces to sue the Yavapai County (central Arizona) Sheriff's office in an effort to have them release information related to the deaths of the nineteen hotshot firefighters who died during the Yarnell AZ forest fire. They wanted autopsy data, death location photos, and the descriptions of recovered personal effects. Wisely the sheriff refused to offer up these items to the press. His well-reasoned rationale was to protect the privacy of the grieving widows, near relatives, and (*especially*) the offspring of the hotshots. He had been made aware that the women involved did not want to have their children hearing any grisly details about their fathers or brothers from the other school children.

Somehow the executives at the newspaper and the television station thought that they had a right to the accumulated 'public' information. In an effort to set up a sympathetic defense of their actions, they said that their corporations would "use discretion" in what they would release to the public. Does anyone believe that this type of yellow journalism has justifiable rights just because there are overly curious people who crave their garbage?

Late in 2013 the aforementioned consortium gave up on its court efforts to force the sheriff to release the desired items. Apparently the subsequent black eye that they received from the public had an effect on their civic attitude.

Beware Of Upgrades

When I receive an offer to upgrade an installed piece of freeware, I wonder how much of the new coding is devoted to improving the product and how much of it is directed at privacy invading "nagware" (*popup solicitations to upgrade to a pro version for example*). One update of an anti-malware software has reverted to issuing daily nags about upgrading or adding paid features, in contrast to their previous monthly-only or on-reboot schedule for these items. As a result of that annoyance I dropped the product.

If one is not circumspect about paying attention to each new version during its installation, it may…
...install easily-ignored 'opt-out' toolbars
...change your browser's home page
…put toolbars in your browser
...add other pieces of software that are either unwanted or unsafe

More than once I have had to uninstall offending software to rid my computer from the 'nuisanceware' that came unannounced with it. Sometimes this additional software embeds itself so deeply into the computer's innards that a few of my stockpile of highly specialized cleansing products were required to get the software removed. In one case I had to revert to editing the computer's Registry, which has tens of thousands of entries.

Fortunately for me, I have thirty plus years of dealing with computer ills to fall back on. My sympathies go out to those who don't. Still, on rare occasions I have had to completely flush the computer's operating system and reinstall it and all of my application software in order to get back to normal… a <u>very</u> time consuming process.

After downloading and installing one of the more secretly malicious freeware products, I immediately began receiving junk mail that continues to this day in spite of reporting it to a government site. So much for expecting the government to follow through with their implied assistance.

Trying to unsubscribe to these senders of garbage only serves to guarantee that you will receive even more junk mail in the future. In doing so you have now verified your email address to these bad guys. That pointless exercise would also likely result in having your address being sold to other bad guys. Then your best option may be to abandon the old email address and create a new one. Hopefully your contact list is up to date so that you can notify one and all of that change.

Beware Of Email

In most cases, merely opening a piece of email won't send your world crashing down. You have to click a malicious link or open a tainted email attachment to get into trouble. So be wary of clicking emailed links, and don't open attachments without ensuring their cleanliness. Your antivirus software may activate an anti-malware feature before you can open your email. Look for this option.

I received a series of "no subject" emails from a neighbor which I immediately deleted unopened, suspecting that there was something wrong. Later he sent out a warning message to those in his address book that he had been hacked. My reply to him (*as politely as I could*) was that this problem occurred due to some action that he had taken, and that he may want to hone in on the cause to prevent it from happening in the future. It is not uncommon that this type of situation is the result of poor judgment about opening Internet links, which in his case resulted in a stolen email list, and more.

I have advocated forever to friends that they should never click on any links at known or unknown web sites, or on links of any kind that are sent to them by friends. The chance of infecting ones computer with this action is substantial. The only exception to this rule might be an attachment that you know was created by the sender... such as photos. But then you may never be positive as to the contents in advance without contacting the sender prior to opening the link. Their photo of a beautiful sunset, or whatever, could have been created by the bad guys and have malware imbedded in it.

Are Downloads Safe?

Those of us who buy books at traditional shops should be able to expect anonymity from those interests who may want to profile us. But this is turning out not to be the case with the increasingly popular, downloadable books. The purveyors have your email addresses and selection tastes to use as they see fit because the government has yet to protect us with any meaningful extension to privacy laws.

Currently it is unlikely in the extreme that this data will be used in a nefarious way. However, it can certainly contribute to the flood of spam that reaches inboxes or pops up on browsers. Then it may be only a matter of time before our data is marketed to others for their own purposes, just like our 'public' records now are.

Big business's computers have the capacity to store and collate zillions of pieces of information, and they are already being used for that exact purpose. This is not an esoteric exercise on their part. There is money to be made off of it.

A side effect of some Internet downloads is that they may come embedded with various levels of 'adware', whether their own or from other advertisers. This is especially true with sites that offer up ads to support their free software. The companies with integrity generally rely on paid upgrades to a 'pro' version to support their efforts. But there are also a few that sell their souls to scammers and spammers for their twelve pieces of gold.

Is e-banking Safe?

Most of us think that online banking and Internet sales in this country to be as safe as the proverbial vault. But it turns out that billions of dollars have been extracted from unsuspecting business accounts by foreign entities. Nothing is completely safe from these felons.

Hackers have targeted vulnerable businesses with sophisticated 'phishing' probes that may induce accounting personnel to give up valuable data about their company accounts. Then these thieves employ various methods to drain those accounts and wire the money to safety overseas. Of course there is something akin to *complicity* with those employees who give up the company goods unknowingly. I say 'complicity' because these people do not take sufficient care of company passwords and account numbers when they let malware enter their computers.

Another concern that we should have is the trend towards online access to your money that is being pushed by the larger banks. This Internet process is more efficient for them, but it may also be more dangerous for the persons wanting to manage their money. The danger comes in two potential forms. First, it could only be a matter of time before the next bank is hacked... maybe it will be yours. Second, is the eavesdropping on your computer banking activities from a nearby hacker with the right equipment. While both of the situations may rare and be covered by a banks guarantees, it can still result is a short term issue.

Is The Internet Safe?

Do you really need me to tell you that it is not… and that it may never be? Behind every click you make can lurk some entity that is trying to take advantage of your lack of understanding of the dangers involved.

One simple 'tell' that gives away a phishing site is that the URL (*Internet address*) doesn't match the URL of the website you think it is. Intentional misspelling is used to trap the casual user. If the spelling of a nasty website like fasebook.com or paypall.com, for example, and asks for your login data… beat a quick retreat. Always give the URL of a website that asks you to log in a close examination before you enter your password.

Most social media and banking websites use HTTPS encryption by default. If the site that you're visiting doesn't have the lock icon next to its URL in your browser, that's a good sign that there is something amiss.

To help you avoid the plethora of sophisticated phishing expeditions which are aimed at stealing your personal information, you could employ website rating software like McAfee Site Advisor, Web of Trust, or others. They generally attach to your browser and monitor your Internet activity when heading to a website, but in a good way. Not only can they rank sites from safe to unsafe, but they may also put up a warning screen when a selected site is deemed particularly dangerous. I have found that the negative ratings which may be supplied are not always right on target with their warning, however it is far better to be safe than sorry.

Then there are those sites which offer enticing offers to the unwary (*trips, discounts, and free stuff*) that are primarily designed to extract personal information from you that you give them freely for "the chance of a lifetime" or some such enticement. For example, one particular site offers to supply you with your free credit rating score. But when you go to its site, it asks for unnecessary data about you (*as far as your credit rating is concerned*). Presumably this personal information is then bundled with the valuable tidbits from thousands or millions of others. The subsequent buyers of this data, in their turn, may use that information to target the unwary for spam. So remember... there's no free lunch. You won't win the house or vacation anyway, so why help out the spam industry?

Another danger is the fake update or error message. Some of these may simply ask you to update a program that you have or have not installed. At the extreme end of this issue are sites that issue a false warning about your computer that they can fix with by just clicking on [OK]. [OK], of course, allows them to enter your computer with their poison. The adverse effects of clicking may not surface for some time, making a determination what the problem is more difficult to identify.

When doing an internet search based on looking for a particular software brand based on keyword(s), you may be confronted with a number of sites that appear to offer the same information. This can be deceptive. Be sure to check the URL that is under the heading to make sure that you are headed to the correct site. For example, a URL that is "microsoft.something.com" will not take you to Microsoft. It will take you to "something.com". The Internet is filled with these bogus look-alikes, and some supply malicious viruses.

Social Media Sites

With the explosion in social networking sites and the millions of daily post-ers, a vast, lucrative arena has become available to the data aggregators. They sift through this fertile territory for the morsels of information on anyone foolish enough to expose themselves to the public. Virtually every piece of personal information that is posted there can be extracted, analyzed, packaged, sold, combined with other data, repackaged, and resold many times over.

The buyers of these packages mostly use the data to target you for advertising when you visit websites. This might not be all that bad if that is where it stopped. Federal agencies have also been known to buy into this invasion of privacy for whatever suits their purposes. This is probably why there have been no effective statutes dealing with the issue.

Facebook, YouTube, Google+, and other social networking sites are perceived by many, I suppose, to pose no real threat to anyone. Many people use them for entertainment and communication. After all, the innocent data on these sites has been given up voluntarily by the user. But every piece of that information is being digitized (*much like Goggle's Internet search records*) and is available to be sold to the aggregators if (*when*) they so choose to do so. Then those folks, one level removed from the original data source, are not so easily restricted in how they can manipulate and sell personal information, or to whom they can sell.

Google has had a change of policy whereby if you install some of their software, you are automatically enrolled in Google+ without your permission. Then, they may even post personal information from your Facebook wall, such as any blogs that they may have uncovered. This invasion is, of course, intended to target your Internet searches with 'appropriate' ads, which generate massive revenue for Google. We're talking billions of dollars folks, so you can see why this activity is perpetuated. Apparently being a monster sized company is not enough for those with a voracious appetite for becoming even larger. "Vee vant to ruhl das vorld".

When I elected to install Google World (a 3D mapping program) some time back, it immediately tried to install their Google Chrome, browser, on my computer without my permission. Only quick action on my part stopped this invasion from occurring. While Chrome may or may not be an excellent browser, it will never find a place on my computer because of their unscrupulous, in my opinion, tactics.

Google in particular pays numerous software vendors to include the Chrome browser with their offerings. Usually this takes the form of a check-box that must be discovered and then unchecked in order to prevent that action from taking place.

Caution... Facebook(ers)

Facebook Connect is a software product that allows users to log into various websites and apps using their Facebook identity. My first reaction to this 'convenience' was wondering why anyone would choose to give over that amount of control to a known offender of privacy. And my aversion to this giveaway was justified when Facebook made its intention known that it would track connection activities in order to sell to targeted advertisers. Does this come as a surprise to anyone?

As reported on television news, a high school teacher ran into the arrogance of Facebook when she posted derogatory opinions about her school's administrative staff and some of her students. She posted the comments on her Facebook account, and marked then "for friends only". Subsequently, she discovered that that information went public when Facebook changed her privacy settings without her advise and consent.

I do not know if the Facebook site users had been informed of this unilateral change, but this particular teacher was not aware of it. As a result of her comments getting back to the school and to the student's parents, she was asked to resign her position, and is now in financial distress. Are you getting that you can not trust social networks to act in your best interests? It's all about the amount of revenue that they can generate.

Have you ever applied for a job that you thought you were well qualified for, and then failed to receive an offer? One possible reason for this could be what has been posted online about you, not just by yourself, but also by others. The information may not be fair or even accurate, but for some companies it has become a resource by which to make judgments an applicant. So the minor high that you may receive from "talking" about yourself can become a real downer.

Of course we have all read-about/heard-about the profusion of identify theft that takes in billions of dollars per year from the naïve or those who fail to protect themselves. By now we should all know how important it is that we shred our documents rather than just trashing them, and not leaving mail in the mailbox overnight.

In spite of oft-repeated caveats about exposing personal information, there are millions of post-ers who want every detail of their boring(?) lives broadcast far and wide over the social networks. Undoubtedly this has something to do with our receiving a mild brain high of endorphin (*no kidding*) when we talk about ourselves. But no good act goes unpunished. On some occasions the bad guys have taken to extracting this 'inside' information to impersonate bloggers to their older, less sophisticated relatives. Then they invent a horror story that the person needs emergency money for some semi-believable reason. Finally they asked to have it sent ASAP, before their fictitious story can be verified. This is a technique that works often enough to make the presumably time-consuming data-culling and thousands of telephone calls worthwhile.

According to a news article, a young woman met her soul mate from postings she uncovered on Facebook. To me this is like looking for a renter on Craig's List, where scammers and sleaze have been known to hang out. So she met up with this pedophile and is now missing... either being a run-away (*less likely*) or having been kidnapped and presumably killed (*more likely*).

So if a young adult, who should have known better, can be conned into meeting someone offers themselves on the Internet... someone with qualifications that are straight out of their imagination, what chance will gullible children have to protect themselves? The answer is very little because of the vicarious thrills that might come with communications between strangers. Young people, especially, need to have a mentor that spells out the inherent dangers in making "friends" with people that they do not know. There are thousands of predators who are looking for the opportunity to take advantage of, or worse, of the unsuspecting.

Facebook Exposures

On a different tact... like Twitter, Facebook is partnering with news organizations to find and display conversations based on keywords. If people or postings with public profiles talk about specific events, Facebook's partners can embed those conversations into a Public Feed. Their vice president, Justin Osofsky, said media outlets could then show real-time conversations in their news coverage. Facebook is also offering a program to analyze keyword usage, such as...
...how many posts mention a particular word in a certain time frame
...whether the term is more popular among men or women
...what part of the country is talking about that term the most

Then the news partners can include Facebook metrics in their event coverage. These features will be available to media partners, news organizations, and marketing developers yet to be announced. While the metrics aspect may be less harmful that other data culling, what can be said about an outlet's repeating of people's conversations for the purpose of making a buck?

According to Kevin Skapinetz, program director for product strategy at IBM Security Systems, "Social media has become a new playground for attackers". A report also noted that there is a growing trend in the actual, but subtle, takeover [and malicious use] of social media profiles which have a large number of followers. This trend plays a pivotal role in the way attackers are reaching large targets.

"It's one thing to get an email or spam from someone you've never heard of," Skapinetz said in an interview. "It's another thing to have one of your friends have their account compromised and send you *a link that might interest you.* When this perversion of email is used in an attack, it will be under guise of having come from a social media account," he said.

Attackers are becoming more operationally sophisticated. Social media assaults can affect more than the usual suspects, too. These media exploits affect more than just individuals. They can negatively impact enterprise brand reputations, and then cause financial losses, the report went on to say.

Vast numbers of social media post-ers may feel compelled to give up their travel plans to the world… which is only a slight exaggeration. With that data and other information which these foolish people supply, it is not all that difficult for a burglar to locate their home address and, of course, learn when it will be vacant. At that point they might decide that you house is ripe for the picking. And whose fault is that?

Are They For Real?

According to a PC World article, not everyone on Facebook is who they claim to be. And while some of the info posted is nothing more than harmless bragging, some fakers can be downright dangerous to the unsophisticated.

Facebook is willing to admit (*conservatively?*) that 7 percent of their accounts may not be attached to real people at all. Twitter suggests that some 5 percent of their accounts are fraudulent. That's millions of accounts. Whether or not these assessments are on target or not is almost irrelevant. The point is that there are numerous bad guys out there looking to take advantage of the under-educated.

So how can the curious and foolishly-adventurous surfers avoid these fakes? One possible way is to go to 'beehive.com' and check out their social site assessment software. It calculates 'account believability indexes' that may offer an appropriate warning to the wary. For those others who just can't stand not getting involved into other people's lives, good luck.

Caution... Craigslist(ers)

Craigslist has made some strides in protecting its users from Internet predators, but for some hackers they are just a challenge to be surmounted. That's the case with a Trojan program that had been targeted at their online classified advertising service. The malware ends up on computers of the unsuspecting users who click on an infected link, expecting to receive a fictitious update to a real program, for example. After infecting the user's machine, the malware transforms their computer into a zombie for a 'botnet' which makes spam (*or worse*) postings to Craigslist. An Android version of this app can be planted onto a person's phone so all their activities can be monitored.

Scams & Scoundrels

Another deception to become conscious of is the proliferation of telephone scams. I will not try to enumerate even a few of these, but suffice to say that you should never give out personal information to anyone that calls, not matter how valid the request may sound. No legitimate company will ever ask for that personal information via telephone... period. And if you have caller-id, why pick up the phone for a business... or an area code that is not where a friend lives.

I remember a pertinent story in my college studies regarding the compacting of animal society and the subsequent aggression among the animals. The study said that the more deer which occupy a given territory, the more likely it is that they will innately act in a manner that designed to thin a heard. While this behavior may not be conscious thought for us as we understand it, who says that our taking up guns and other weapons at the rate we are is all that conscious. It may actually be an evolutionary reaction to the compression of society and the ills that this closeness can present.

Coincidently there are more than a few of us who have taken this notion of thinning the heard to heart for their own justifications. Hence, the proliferation of terrorism. These people do not aspire to attain a better life based on their actions as we understand it, unless you happen agree with their religious motivations and its cruel outcomes. What these terrorists do not grasp is that killing as a means to an end is a shameful and eventually counterproductive act. Their thought control can not be sustained forever.

On a smaller scale, there a growing cadre of home-grown thugs, malcontents, and lone terrorists who find a need to enact revenge on others for the perceived wrongs to their philosophy or person. Others in this group may simply suffer from being mal-wired at birth, or easily indoctrinated by those who were themselves mal-wired, or corrupted by others.

So with all of these threats to our wellbeing, the government steps in with ever increasing assaults on our privacy. Some of their actions are being justified by the type of events just mentioned. Others flow only from a government person's self interest or their misguided agenda. By *misguided*, I refer to those actions that are alleged to be in the public interest by their initiators when the big picture is not taken into consideration. The most obvious example of this type of oppression would be the government's war on drugs... a thoroughly thoughtless, ineffective, and useless waste of the taxpayer's money.

In addition to the above, there is ever increasing surveillance into what we do, where we go, and with whom it is that we communicate. In 2013 Obama stated at a press conference that we need to give up some freedoms (*my words*) in order to protect ourselves. The problem with this attitude is: who the judges of that action are. As I have written, good and evil are often in the eye of the beholder. And without sufficient safeguards against power seekers, evil will prosper.

By now we should all be aware of the NSA's eavesdropping on billions of conversations in this country and abroad. Their logic is that in an effort to prevent terrorist acts, we have to give up some of our precious privacy. This is just one more chip out of the wall of protection from government intrusion into our lives. It smacks in the face of those safeguards that we deserve and should demand.

Thomas Jefferson, President: *A government big enough to give you everything you want, is strong enough to take everything you have.*

Time will tell what new sources of intrusion will become the norm before an effective resistance is raised. And knowing the psychology of the human brain, multiple crises will be required to wake us up.

In Conclusion...

The irony of being able to peer over the "back fence", so to speak, into your neighbor's windows is that a greater number of them can look back at you. And a percentage of these viewers have larceny in their hearts.

Perhaps social networking with strangers and so-called "friends" is nothing more than a fad that will in time grow weary. For me, it has been boring (*and risky*) from the start.

We may not hesitate to caution our children about the dangers of being approached by strangers, but we may also be unwilling take our own good advice when it comes to the Internet.

Wouldn't it be nice if people had the same curiosity about the stealthy maneuvers that their congresspersons are up to as they do about friends and strangers? Maybe we wouldn't be subjected to the degree of political corruption that permeates our government (*and goes on virtually unabated*). That is if people became aware of what is happening because they started paying attention. Alas, this is no doubt wishful thinking on my part.

On the subject of government malfeasance, you may want to check out my book "Pathetic Politics & Performance".

Kip's Books & Links

The books listed here are available in ebook format for Kindle™ and Nook™ readers at Amazon.com and elsewhere. Some of the shorter materials are "ideas" booklets or excerpts from longer books. Hard copy books are available at Createspace.com. The URL links, where listed, access book previews.

A BETTER BATHROOM - An Ideas Guide
Construction
https://www.createspace.com/Preview/1134187
$1.99   34 pages

A BETTER KITCHEN - An Ideas Guide
Construction
https://www.createspace.com/Preview/1134190
$1.99   36 pages

AGGRESSION & BULLYING - It's Not Just Our Wiring
Human Nature
$1.49   11 pages

AN OUTDOOR KITCHEN - The Latest Trend?
Construction
$1.49   6 pages

BEFORE STARTING HOME CONSTRUCTION - What You Need To Know In Advance
Construction
https://www.createspace.com/Preview/4136208
$2.99/$5.49   40 pages

BRAIN CHOICES & FREE WILL - Getting To Know Ourselves Using Concepts That Are Not Well Understood Or Accepted
Human Nature
https://www.createspace.com/Preview/1134191
$3.99/$5.99   78 pages

CUSTOM HOME DOs & DON'Ts - The ULTIMATE Guide To Getting Your Custom Home DONE RIGHT!
Construction
https://www.createspace.com/Preview/1134192
$6.99/10.49   266 pages

DECEPTION IN AMERICA - How We Are Manipulated Big Business, Politicians, The Press & Our Indoctrinations

Government/Business/Politics
https://www.createspace.com/Preview/1134195
$9.99/15.99   458 pages

EVOLUTION, THE BRAIN, & RELIGION - How Evolution Made Us What We Are
Human Nature
https://www.createspace.com/Preview/1134196
$4.99/$6.99   160 pages

EXCESSIVE EXECUTIVE COMPENSATION - What You Should Know About
The Fleecing Of America By Executives & Boards
Government/Business/Politics
$1.49   11 pages

FOLLOWING THE CROWD - How We Fall In Line With Others
Human Nature
$1.49   14 pages

FUN WITH APPETIZERS - For Those Who Like To Entertain Well
Cookbook
https://www.createspace.com/Preview/4438108
$3.99/$5.99   70 pages

FUN WITH CARBOS - The Cookbook For Those Without A Care
Cookbook
https://www.createspace.com/Preview/4440041
$3.99/$5.99   94 pages

FUN WITH CHICKEN - The Fowl & Seafood Cookbook That Avoids Red Meat
Cookbook
https://www.createspace.com/Preview/4441007
$4.99/$6.99   148 pages

FUN WITH DESSERTS - The - What To Do When The
Meal Is Over - Cookbook
Cookbook
https://www.createspace.com/Preview/4444531
$2.99/$5,49   64 pages

FUN WITH ENTREES - Getting To The Heart Of Cooking
Cookbook
https://www.createspace.com/Preview/1135491
$5.99/$8.99   172 pages

FUN WITH MEAT - The Carnivore's Cookbook
Cookbook

https://www.createspace.com/Preview/4436803
$3.99/$5.99   110 pages

FUN WITH SALADS - My Take On The Classics & Others
https://www.createspace.com/Preview/1136150
$1.99/$5.49   24 pages

FUN WITH SEAFOOD – See Food & Eat It Cookbook
Cookbook
https://www.createspace.com/Preview/4494327
$3.99/$5.99   84 pages

FUN WITH SOUP - It's Economical, & Healthy As Well
Cookbook
https://www.createspace.com/Preview/4442511
$1.99/$5.49   38 pages

FUN WITH WINE - Aging And Tasting Wine
$1.49   9 pages
An informative guide, including wine-term explanations.

GOVERNMENT FOR PEOPLE? - How the US government "functions" without regard for the negative ramifications of its actions
Government/Business/Politics
https://www.createspace.com/Preview/1134204
$3.99/$5.99   88 pages

HOME DESIGN GOALS - Important Considerations
Construction
https://www.createspace.com/Preview/1134209
$1.99/$5.49   36 pages

HOME GREEN HOME - The Ins & Outs Of Home Efficiency
Construction
https://www.createspace.com/Preview/1134208
$2.99/$5.49   42 pages

HOW BUSINESS FAILS US - What You Need To Know About Business Corruption
Government/Business/Politics
https://www.createspace.com/Preview/1134206
$2.99/$5.49   70 pages

HOW WE LEARN, WHY WE DON'T - Getting To Know Ourselves
https://www.createspace.com/Preview/1134212
$3.99/$5.99   86 pages

INCONVENIENT REALITY - How Big Business Shoots Us In The Foot, & How Congress And The Press Helped Get Us Into This Mess
https://www.createspace.com/Preview/1134213
Government/Business/Politics
$5.99/$8.99   190 pages

INVADING YOUR PRIVACY - What You Don't Know And What You Should Know
Government/Business/Politics
$1.49   18 pages

LAW IS FOR LAWYERS - The People That We Rely On For Our Protection Can Be The Biggest Offenders Of It
Government/Business/Politics
$1.99   22 pages

ONE POT CLASSICS - The Comfort Food & Easy Clean-up Cookbook
Cookbook
https://www.createspace.com/Preview/1134289
$6.99/$11.49   306 pages

PATHETIC POLITICS & PERFORMANCE - What We Should Know About Our System Of Government
Government/Business/Politics
https://www.createspace.com/Preview/1134290
$4.99/6.99   112 pages

POWER BREEDS ABUSE - Or To Put This Another Way... On Some Level, Power Always Leads To Corruption
Government/Business/Politics
https://www.createspace.com/Preview/1134291
$2.99/4.99   48pages

SELECTING A CONTRACTOR - Making The Right Choice The First Time
Construction
$1.49   11 pages

SELLING & STAGING A HOME - Getting The Most From Your Efforts
Construction
$1.49   6 pages

SENIOR FRIENDLY HOME DESIGN - Making A House Safe
Construction
$1.49   11 pages

SOCIAL NETWORKING - The Downside To Exposing Yourself
Human Nature
$1.49   5 pages

THE PRESS'S ROLE IN BAD POLITICS - What They Do, And How They Contribute
Government/Business/Politics
https://www.createspace.com/Preview/1134295
$1.99/$5.49   32 pages

THE WAR ON DRUGS - How It Harms Everyone
Government/Business/Politics
$1.49   6 pages

TO SELL OR REMODEL - Making The Right Decision
Construction
$1.99   9 pages

TRAVEL DEALS & BARGINS – Gaming The System To Win
Travel
$1.49   14pages

www.ingramcontent.com/pod-product-compliance
Lightning Source LLC
Chambersburg PA
CBHW030553290526
45786CB00004B/1996